SEQUENCING STORIES

Planting a Garden

MEG GAERTNER

The Child's World®
childsworld.com

Published by The Child's World®
1980 Lookout Drive • Mankato, MN 56003-1705
800-599-READ • www.childsworld.com

Photographs ©: Steve Debenport/
iStockphoto, cover (left), cover (middle left),
cover (middle right), cover (right), 3 (top), 3
(bottom), 5, 6, 9, 10, 13, 14, 17, 18, 21

ISBN 9781503835115
LCCN 2018962888

Printed in the United States of America
PA02425

About the Author

Meg Gaertner is a children's book author and editor who lives in Minnesota. When not writing, she enjoys dancing and spending time outdoors.

CONTENTS

Gardening Time! . . . 4

Gardening Time!

Marcus usually likes school. His teacher often plans fun classes. Today's class is special. Today, he and his friends get to plant a garden!

What is your favorite
part of school?

5

Many plants start as seeds. Then they grow into seedlings.

Before they can start planting, the class learns about plants. Marcus's teacher talks to them about plants. She explains what plants need to grow.

Now it is time to begin planting.
First, the gardener helps the students dig
and turn the soil. This loosens the
soil. One girl grabs a shovel.
Another girl uses a **spade**.

Different tools do different jobs in the garden.

9

Planting in garden boxes can keep out weeds and pests.

While the teacher helps other students, Marcus gets to work. He uses a garden **hoe** to even out the soil.

Soon, the ground is ready. The teacher brings over a plant. She shows Marcus how to put the plant in the ground.

Fun Fact

Sometimes people plant seeds. They can also buy young plants at the store.

Always touch plants gently.

13

Marcus must bury the plant's roots so it can grow.

After that, Marcus adds soil around the plant. He pats down the soil. He wants the plant to stand tall.

Then, it is time to water the plant.

Marcus fills a watering can with water.

He pours the water onto all of the plants

in the garden. Finally, the planting

is done.

Too little or too much water makes plants droop.

17

Some plants take all summer to grow.

18

Plants take a long time to grow. Marcus and his friends return to the garden from time to time. They pull weeds. They water the plants. They see how the plants are growing.

After a long time, the plants are ready to **harvest**. Marcus picks vegetables from the garden. He can't wait to eat them later!

Fun Fact

There are vegetable gardens, flower gardens, and even rock gardens.

What is your favorite vegetable to eat?

21

Glossary

harvest (HAR-vist) To harvest something is to collect it or gather it up. Marcus and his friends harvest the vegetables when they are ready.

hoe (HOH) A hoe is a gardening tool with a thin blade and a long handle. Marcus uses a hoe to loosen the dirt.

nutrients (NOO-tree-uhnts) Nutrients are something that living things need to stay strong and healthy. Important plant nutrients are found in soil.

roots (ROOTS) The roots are the part of a plant that grows in the ground. Roots can grow most easily in loose soil.

spade (SPAYD) A spade is a gardening tool with a flat blade and a long handle. Gardeners may use a spade to dig up the soil.

To Learn More

BOOKS

Barger, Jeff. *How to Make a Terrarium*.
Vero Beach, FL: Rourke Educational Media, 2018.

Bell, Samantha S. *Build a Compact Garden*.
Mankato, MN: The Child's World, 2017.

Rattini, Kristin Baird. *Seed to Plant*.
Washington, DC: National Geographic, 2014.

WEBSITES

Visit our website for links about planting a garden:
childsworld.com/links

Note to Parents, Teachers, and Librarians: We routinely verify our Web links to make sure they are safe and active sites. So encourage your readers to check them out!

Index